The Colonial Search
for a Southern Eden

The Colonial Search
for a Southern Eden

By LOUIS B. WRIGHT

THE UNIVERSITY OF ALABAMA PRESS
Tuscaloosa

∞
The paper on which this book is printed meets the minimum
requirements of American National Standard for Information Science—
permanence of Paper for Printed Library Materials, ANSI Z39.48-1984.

Library of Congress Cataloging-in-Publication Data

Wright, Louis B. (Louis Booker), 1899–
  The colonial search for a southern Eden / by Louis B. Wright.
      p. cm.
  Three lectures delivered at the Dancy Foundation, Alabama College, Apr.
29–May 1, 1951.
  Includes bibliographical references.
  ISBN 0-8173-5180-9 (pbk. : alk. paper)
  1. Southern States—Economic conditions—17th century. 2. Great
Britain—Colonies—America—Commerce. I. Title.
  HC107.A13W7 2005
  330.975'02--dc22
                                        2005041757

Preface

THE THREE LECTURES printed here are reproduced as delivered at Alabama College in the spring of 1951 under the provisions of a bequest left by Unity Dandridge Dancy. They represent an interpretation of the persistent dream which influenced England to seek to establish profitable colonies in the Southern region of the Atlantic seaboard. Designed as lectures for a general audience, they can make no pretense to treat definitively a subject requiring a large volume.

The writer wishes to express his profound appreciation to Dr. John T. Caldwell, president of Alabama College, and to his faculty for their gracious hospitality.

L.B.W.

July 1, 1951
Folger Library
Washington, D. C.

Contents

I

The Elizabethan Dream
of Wealth

DURING THE PAST DECADE patriots of sundry sorts have
exhorted Americans to study our history. A few years
ago the *New York Times* made an investigation of the
average American's knowledge of history and discovered
that he had a mind discouragingly innocent of any taint
of historical knowledge. Other investigators, professional
and amateur, looked into the matter and exploded with
alarming generalizations about our ignorance. Many an
American couldn't say whether Old Hickory was a brand
of liquor or a variety of smoked ham. A considerable
number thought Christopher Columbus was an orchestra
leader and Zachary Taylor a movie actor. The majority
of people questioned were positive that Daniel Webster
wrote the dictionary. A surprising number thought
Tammany Hall was a place in New York where prize
fights were held, but others contended that the Tweed
Ring was the scene of such encounters. Some declared
that the free silver movement was a campaign to raise
money for the Red Cross. But perhaps the zenith of
innocence was reached by the college boy who reported

that the Missouri Compromise was a newspaper published in St. Louis.

Exposures of American ignorance of history became a sort of pastime, and well-meaning citizens, better informed—they hoped—than the average, began to demand more American history in the schools. In some states the legislatures passed laws requiring college courses in American history for graduation. As high schools, colleges, and universities established new courses, the American Legion, the Daughters of the American Revolution, and other hopeful organizations sat back to contemplate the patriotism which these courses would engender. What the results have been, I have no way of knowing. As a teacher of American history for many years, I can report that some of the courses were ill-conceived and probably defeated their purposes.

But we do need good American history, history which begins a long way back, because the history of the past enables us to see our own times in proper perspective. If official Washington understood history somewhat better, I am convinced that we would have more wisdom in government.

History also provides a great amount of encouragement and consolation for the thoughtful reader. Ever since Adam encountered the archangel after eating the forbidden fruit, mankind has been constantly on the verge of disaster, and yet, somehow, we have managed to survive. If we take the trouble to investigate, we will discover that other ages were strangely like ours, and our ancestors often met and overcame difficulties uncannily like our own. At the present moment particularly we need to remember that our difficulties are not new in the world, and we can endure—and probably survive—as did our ancestors.

In many respects, the Renaissance, if I may use that term of convenience for the sixteenth and seventeenth centuries, faced problems similar to ours. A new science was born and attained an astonishing development in those two centuries. Immense changes took place in the concepts of space and time in relation to the physical universe. The new science introduced infinite complexities, and added new confusions. Medicine, chemistry, physics, and astronomy made advancements which gave them a right to be called modern. Technology altered the living conditions of millions of men and women. Military and naval science changed the modes of warfare and increased the potentials for man's destruction of man. The improvement in artillery and small arms in these two centuries and the control of the explosive effects of gunpowder was as epoch-making as the use of atomic fission.

The geography of the world completely changed, and with it came a change in men's imaginations. The discoveries in the New World must have seemed as marvelous—and as incredible—as the possibilities of interplanetary voyages today. Certainly the imaginings of the authors of what we call "science fiction" are hardly less fantastic than the tales which travellers brought back from the New World.

To understand our own times we must begin our study of American history at least with the age of Elizabeth, for that age saw the development of many of the ideas, the social, intellectual, and spiritual movements which have determined the quality of the English-speaking world in later generations. Since our time is limited, I want to concentrate upon a single theme, the motivations for, and implications of, colonization in what is now the Southern United States.

The English were slow to take part in the partition of the newly discovered lands. Many reasons account for this. When Columbus first sighted the West Indies, England had not yet recovered from the Wars of the Roses, and Henry VII was still busy trying to make secure the throne which he had seized seven years before from Richard III. It would take almost another century for England to gather strength to demand its place among the great European powers. During that century, Spain would dominate Europe, threaten England, and occupy those portions of the New World which she considered the most fruitful.

But when English seamen defeated the Spanish Armada in 1588, they established England's position, not only as a naval power, but as a contender for a part of the New World which Spain had previously claimed. A few years before, England had made tentative efforts to gain a foothold in America. We are all familiar with Sir Walter Raleigh's colonial ventures, his ill-fated colony on Roanoke Island, and his dreams of an English empire across the seas. These schemes, however, had provoked controversies at home—controversies which do not sound unfamiliar to presentday Americans—and England's decisive efforts in the New World had to wait for nearly twenty years after the Armada.

Raleigh's dreams of overseas expansion aroused the fears of what we would call the isolationist faction in politics. For example, so shrewd a man as Lord Burghley, Queen Elizabeth's great secretary, believed that England's proper destiny was to avoid over-extending herself, keep out of entanglements in the New World, develop trade with the countries across the Channel, and grow peacefully prosperous. It was a very tempting doctrine, as isolationism always is. The trouble with this view was that it was short-sighted and ultimately impossible of attainment.

Raleigh's group realized that not only England's prosperity but, in the end, England's survival, depended upon access to America with its new wealth, new sources of raw materials, new markets, and its strategic opportunities for curtailing the power of Spain, the country which most Englishmen believed to be the greatest threat to the liberties of free men. Eventually Raleigh's views prevailed, but his inveterate opposition to Spain caused a crass appeaser, King James I, to send him to the scaffold in 1618 (on a trumped-up charge of treason) in an effort to placate the Spanish king.

The English expansionists were undoubtedly right in their belief that at all costs they must wrest some of the New World from Spain. The gold and silver of Mexico and Peru had enriched Spain and given it the financial power to support fleets and armies which kept most of Europe in fear or subjection. To be sure, English corsairs, of whom John Hawkins and Francis Drake are the best-remembered examples, from time to time captured rich galleons and even waylaid whole treasure fleets, but these forays were hardly more important than the accidental breaks in an oil pipeline which occasionally interrupt the delivery of fuel. Not only Englishmen but other thoughtful enemies of Spain realized that the greatest damage to Spanish power could be caused by stopping the flow of wealth from America. The year before Jamestown was settled, a Flemish refugee in Holland, Willem Usselinx, recommended that the Dutch organize a West India Company which would establish outposts on the flanks of Spain's lines of communication and seize the wealth as it flowed from America. Thus Dutch Calvinists would serve God and country and enrich themselves. Years before, Englishmen had made similar recommendations.

Richard Hakluyt, editor of the classic collection of travel narratives, was the greatest propagandist of his age for English expansion. As early as 1580 he had prepared a paper entitled "A Discourse of the Commodity of the Taking of the Straits of Magellanus," which emphasized the danger to England and the rest of Protestant Europe if Spain were allowed to dominate the New World.[1] With the shrewdness of a modern devotee of geopolitics, he advised the Queen to garrison and fortify both ends of the Straits of Magellan, and to establish a fortress on Cape St. Vincent in Brazil. If this might seem too bold a venture, he suggested a cunning device. Let a certain pirate of his acquaintance, one Clerke by name, establish these strongholds with arms and men supplied secretly by the English government. In this way the English could maintain their innocence and at the same time trouble Spain. Four years later in

1584, Hakluyt, encouraged by Raleigh and his group of expansionists, prepared a longer paper, known today as the *Discourse of Western Planting,* and presented it in person to Queen Elizabeth.

Raleigh at this time was trying to establish his colony in North Carolina, and Hakluyt was urging vigorous support of a national policy which would look toward an English barrier in the South against any further advancement of Spain northward. In essence Hakluyt proposed that England plant colonies along the American coast north of Florida, fortify naval bases from which she could harass Spanish communications with the West Indies and Mexico, and search for a northwest passage to China.

Motives for the increasing English interest in the New World were mixed—and all are interesting to the student of our origins. Both clergy and statesmen were concerned about the souls of the Indians, and many a parson proclaimed from the pulpit the calamities which were certain to follow if Protestant England stood idly by and allowed Spain to convert the heathen to Roman Catholicism. Certain statesmen joined the clergy in the endeavor to arouse their countrymen to the necessity of making Protestants out of as many red men as possible. We must never forget that religion and politics were inextricably mingled in this age, as in others. The religious motive in colonization has been often overlooked and deserves more emphasis than it has received. Much of this missionary zeal was genuine and must not be discounted as merely cynical self-interest. Many expansionists shared Hakluyt's genuine piety.

Although the average Englishman may not have paid much attention to the high politics of checkmating Spain by establishing bases in the New World, he was acutely aware of the potentialities of American wealth. Then as now the European's primary interest in America was determined by the economic benefits he expected to derive from the new country. Apprentices and schoolboys dreamed of going to sea and coming back with Spanish gold in their pockets. In every port town, sailors swaggered and spent prize money with the extravagance which comes with easy money in any age. Shrewd merchants in London and Bristol invested in very dubious voyages and sometimes had immense profits to show for their risk capital. The Queen herself took a cut from every buccaneer who could not evade government spies and officers.

The story of Drake's voyage around the world in 1577-80, and of the enormous riches which he brought back in the "Golden Hind," soon echoed through all England. His sailors, enriched with a share of the spoils, told their adventures in taverns, on the wharfs, and in the market places, and their stories whetted the appetites of other Englishmen for similar opportunities. One Henry Robarts, himself a sailor, trader, and self-appointed poet laureate of such seafarers, wrote a poem glorifying the expedition when Drake set out in 1585 for another foray into Spanish territory. This poem, entitled *A most friendly farewell, Giuen by a welwiller to the right worshipful Sir Frauncis Drake, Knight . . . with an Incouragement to all his saylers and souldiers to be forward in this honourable exploite* (1585), praised

Drake and others like him who had made the West Indies tributary to English buccaneers. Complaining that other writers had not sufficiently appreciated the great deeds of Drake, his hero, Robarts undertook to immortalize the man who had become such a byword in Spain that mothers frightened their children by the mere mention of his name.[2]

The sheer love of adventure, plus the hope of quick riches, lured Englishmen from all the maritime districts to put to sea. Merchants in London, Bristol, Plymouth, and other ports, country gentlemen, courtiers, and even an occasional well-heeled bishop, invested in privateering expeditions. Procuring letters of marque from the English authorities, or in some instances from the French, they fitted out fast ships, well-armed and manned with crews ready for any deed. These vessels roamed the seas in search of prey and their captains were never too squeamish about their conduct. They brought in gold, silver, and jewels from Spanish America, which acted as a further stimulant to English hopes of expansion overseas—and, incidentally, accelerated a creeping inflation which had been gaining headway since the beginning of the sixteenth century.

A vessel so fabulously rich that memories of its capture still linger in West Country folklore was brought into Dartmouth harbor in 1592 by a swarm of privateers. The vessel was the "Madre de Dios," sixteen hundred tons burden, one of the largest carracks in the Spanish merchant service, homeward bound from the East Indies. Her holds were stuffed with spices, perfumes, drugs, silks, cottons, carpets, finely-wrought jewelry, gold, silver, pearls, diamonds, rubies, and other precious luxuries. Walter Raleigh, who had been one of the heaviest investors in the syndicate of privateers which captured the ship, was at the time a prisoner in the Tower, lodged there by a jealous Queen for marrying one of her prettiest maids-of-honor. News of the arrival of the "Madre de Dios" quickly spread as sailors, ship-captains, and investors quarreled over the division of the spoil. Since Raleigh, the idol of the West Country sailors, was the only man who could bring order out of the chaos, the Queen released him from prison to go to Dartmouth and see what he could salvage for the Crown.

Raleigh tried to make a fair division between seamen, commanders, and the backers of the expedition, always mindful to give the Queen a lion's share. In so doing he won release from the Tower. Some of the cargo was transferred to London by water, but bullock carts groaned for days with the freight sent overland. Many plain seamen, fresh from the farms and villages of Devon, came home from this buccaneering expedition literally with fortunes in their breeches pockets, sometimes in diamonds and pearls filched from the treasure before Raleigh's arrival. The richness of this vessel with the sacred name became a byword, and its capture sent uncounted expeditions into the western seas in the expectation of finding a similar treasure trove.

The goods of the "Madre de Dios" were a concrete illustration of the wealth from overseas. It made little difference that these particular commodities came from the Far East. Overseas lay the sources of wealth and ease for innumerable Englishmen, both great men at court and simple fellows who might leave the plow for a trick at sea. Before long America and Asia would be inextricably linked in the ramifications of overseas expansion and what affected one would affect the other. The spoil of the "Madre de Dios" must have suggested this fact to a few thoughtful business men and statesmen in 1592. Within a quarter of a century the fact was self-evident.

Most of the gold and silver brought into England, however, was of American origin, and quick riches from the vast hoards of precious metals believed to exist in America animated the dreams of Elizabethans. The story of the search for gold and silver by the early explorers has been often told, and the relation of these pioneers' single purpose in looking for mineral wealth has sometimes obscured the fact that many thoughtful men among them recognized other forms of wealth which they encountered. Captain John Smith, for example, was quick to realize that furs and codfish might produce more prosperity than gold mines. But the power of gold and silver was undeniable. And the fact that Spanish America produced these commodities in quantities was tangible and self-evident to hundreds of men who had hefted captured treasure chests. Furthermore, as far as Englishmen could ascertain, the best mines were in the southern regions. Consequently it behooved Englishmen to find a spot in the South for a base of operations.

After the failure of Raleigh's attempts at colonization in Virginia, he turned his attention to regions farther south where he believed he would find hoards of gold for himself and his Queen. Furthermore, bases there might give the English greater opportunities for attacking the Spanish possessions. Raleigh's high-vaulting ambition led him to dream of conquering eventually all of the Spanish Empire. This was a political doctrine which he was to maintain until the end of his life. The conquest of the Spanish Empire would bring untold riches to England; and not only riches, for it would give England power the like of which it had never known. It would also gain for Englishmen credit in heaven, because, linked with such a conquest, was the opportunity to carry to the native Indians the benefits of the Protestant faith. The Indians, it was argued, would rush to ally themselves with the English. Since 1583, Englishmen had been able to read a remarkable narrative of the cruelties of the Spaniards toward the Indians, a narrative written by a Spanish priest, himself an eye-witness, Bartolomé de Las Casas. Las Casas' work, translated as *The Spanish Colonie, or Briefe Chronicle of the Acts and Gests of the Spaniardes,* convinced many English politicians and promoters that the Spaniards had prepared the way for their own destruction by alienating the native populations—where indeed, they had not completely eliminated them. Las Casas' vivid descriptions of his countrymen's cruelty became a potent piece of propaganda in the hands of English expansionists.[3]

Putting theory into practice, Raleigh in 1595 made a voyage of discovery to Guiana, a fabled country on the upper reaches of the Orinoco River, in what is now Venezuela. Legend reported that one of the Inca princes had fled from Pizarro's soldiers, carrying tons of Inca gold and silver across the Andes to Guiana. Seated at

Manoa, his capital, a city beside an island sea, this Inca prince ruled the former kingdom of Guiana, a country itself so rich in gold that the precious metal could be scooped up pure from the sands along the creeks and rivers. Indeed, somewhere in the interior, a mountain of pure gold glittered with such a brilliant light that it hurt the eyes of men unaccustomed to its sheen. Since wonders as great as this had proved true, only the most cynical doubted that Guiana might be as rich as Mexico and Peru. Furthermore, the Spaniards had failed to establish permanent settlements on the Orinoco, and for all the Spanish pretensions, it was a virgin country waiting for English occupation.

This country had been named El Dorado, meaning the "gilded," from the reputed habit of the king and his nobles at their feasts to coat their bodies with dust of pure gold. A Spaniard who had penetrated the back-country and had seen all this with his own eyes—or so he said—wrote a letter which Sir Robert Dudley intercepted at Trinidad early in 1595. "For the abundance of gold which he [the Spaniard] saw in the citie [of Manoa]," Raleigh wrote later, "the Images of gold in their Temples, the plates, armors, and shields of gold which they vse in the wars, he called it El Dorado."[4]

Raleigh's expedition did not find the golden city of Manoa, but he and his men heard stories to confirm their belief in the wealth which lay somewhere beyond the point they reached—always just beyond their reach, like the pot of gold at the foot of the rainbow. Although Raleigh himself saw no golden mountain, he heard that further up the Orinoco's tributaries were mountains where the rocks were pure gold. He also got a distant view of a mountain of crystal, perhaps even richer than gold, for it was reported to be covered with diamonds and other precious stones. "I was enformed of the mountaine of Christall, to which in trueth for the length of the way, and the euill season of the yeare, I was not able to march, nor abide any longer vpon the iourney," Raleigh wrote; "we saw it a farre off and it appeared like a white Church towre of an exceeding height. . . . Berreo [a Spanish captain] tolde mee that it hath Diamondes and other precious stones on it, and that they shined very farre off."[5]

The will-o'-the-wisp which was gold, or the glitter of jewels, lured many Elizabethans to risk their lives in explorations in strange lands. They dreamed of easy wealth which they would pick up and bring home. Few of those who ventured their lives returned with any gold, but they managed to establish in English thought a conviction that overseas expansion was desirable and necessary to the national interest.

The publication of Raleigh's *The Discoverie of the large and bewtiful Empire of Guiana* in 1596 created an interest in that region which would last for generations and result in a long sequence of colonizing efforts on the Orinoco. Indeed, the explorations of Raleigh were invoked by Great Britain as late as 1895 in the famous boundary dispute between British Guiana and Venezuela, a dispute which very nearly involved the United States in war with Britain in defense of the Monroe Doctrine. Raleigh's book appealed to human greed by emphasizing the easy riches to be found in Guiana, but it also contains the hint of a new thought, that of other economic interests which England had in a land producing tropical products. "Where there is store of gold," Raleigh commented, "it is in effect nedeles to remember other commodities for trade: but it [Guiana] hath towards the south part of the riuer, great quantities of Brasill woode, and of diuers berries that die a most perfect crimson and Carnation: And for painting, al France, Italy, or the east Indies yeild none such: For the more the skyn is washed, the fayrer the cullour appeareth, and with which, euen those brown and tawnie women spot themselues, and cullour their cheekes. All places yeilde abundance of Cotton, of sylke, of Balsamum, and of those kindes most excellent, and neuer known in Europe: of all sortes of gummes, of Indian pepper: and what else the countries may afforde within the land wee knowe not, neither had we time to abide the triall, and search. The soile besides is so excellent and so full of riuers, as it will carrie sugar, ginger, and all those other commodities, which the west Indies hath." Here we have mention of silk, cotton, pepper, sugar, dye-stuffs, rare woods, ginger, and other commodities which western Europe, with a fresh appetite for luxuries, found desirable—all commodities which England could not produce but had to buy from outside its domain.

Although mania for gold as an incentive to overseas enterprise did not end with Raleigh's expedition of 1595, gradually the idea of the profits from trade and the production of exotic commodities within a colonial framework came to dominate the thinking of the expansionists. Raleigh himself, whose enemies among the pro-Spanish faction managed to have him sentenced to death and confined to the Tower late in 1603, made a second voyage to Guiana. Appealing to the cupidity of the Scottish king, Raleigh received a warrant to leave the Tower in 1617 to search once more for the golden city of Manoa. The voyage ended in disaster. Raleigh lost his son in the expedition and came back to his own execution on Tower Hill. By this time, however, times had changed in more ways than one. English business men and investors were thinking of colonies as sources of trade and commerce, rather than as mines of gold and silver bullion.

By an odd paradox, the rapid expansion of English commerce in the Far East had dismayed some of the expansionists themselves, and helped to focus attention more acutely on southern colonies in America. When Queen Elizabeth chartered the fraternity of the East India Company on December 31, 1600, she began a chain of events which would change the history of the world. Soon investors in the East India Company were bringing home cargoes of rich merchandise which England had formerly procured in trade with Venice, Genoa, Portugal, and Spain. But these were luxuries like silk, cotton, spices, dyes, sugar, and other exotic products. To procure these goods, English merchants had to pay out gold and silver bullion, and the economists of the day began to cry ruin. The drain of money from the kingdom was more than the country could stand, they argued. Satirists ridiculed the taste for luxuries, preachers railed against extravagance, and pamphleteers in the early seventeenth century declared that the East India Company was bringing disaster on the country. A faction of patriotic Englishmen, concerned about the welfare of the economy, clamored for a source of exotic commodities within the dominion of English governance, colonies where Englishmen might produce this wealth for themselves without draining funds from the kingdom.

Throughout the seventeenth century, and later, the official favor of the English government was lavished on the southern colonies of the plantation type rather than upon the commercial colonies of New England. Indeed, during most of the colonial period, England regarded New England with considerable suspicion and distrust, for New England was a commercial competitor with the mother country, and the merchants of Boston and Salem were not too observant of the Navigation Acts, designed to regulate trade for the advantage of English merchants. The interest which England showed in the Southern colonies as opposed to those in the North continued long after the colonial period, and was almost sufficient to persuade England to intervene in behalf of the Southern Confederacy in 1861. The reasons for this continued interest we shall discuss later.

Despite the desire of James I to keep peace with Spain, he did not go so far as to discourage colonization in the South. The first permanent English settlement at Jamestown in 1607 was regarded by the Spanish interests as a threat, and the Spanish ambassador busied himself with intrigues against the promoters of the Virginian enterprise, all to no avail. English promoters in this period also made repeated efforts to establish colonies on the Orinoco, and even in the Amazon valley. For a time the Pilgrim fathers were almost persuaded that they ought to seek refuge in Guiana, but at last decided in favor of the north part of Virginia, landing by misadventure, as we know, at Plymouth. The Bermudas, or the Sommers Islands, were settled under a charter granted in 1615, and quickly showed a profit from the production of tobacco. A minister, Lewis Hughes, writing in 1621 from Bermuda stressed "the goodnes of God, in reseruing and keeping these Ilands, euer since the beginning of the world, for the English Nation, and in not discouering them to any, to inhabit but to the English."[6] In 1627 English colonists occupied Barbados, an island which became a shining example of the wealth to be had from the production of exotic crops, tobacco, cotton, indigo, and later sugar. By 1640, this island supported 18,000 inhabitants. When the spread of the plantation system of sugar production made small farms unprofitable, settlers from Barbados emigrated to other colonies and helped to make them prosperous. A Barbadian, for instance, introduced the cultivation of indigo to South Carolina.

Raleigh's dream of wealth and power through the conquest of the Spanish Empire to the South died hard. Although the first two Stuart kings for the most part tried to avoid undue provocation of Spain, the rise of Oliver Cromwell brought the Spanish problem into sharper focus. The Puritans hated the Catholic power, and Cromwell returned to the policy advocated by Raleigh, using some of the same propaganda which Raleigh and Hakluyt had employed. A scheme to conquer the decaying Spanish Empire by driving against Panama and the West Indies resulted in 1654 in the despatch of an army and naval force believed strong enough to sweep the Caribbean. Ill-luck dogged the expedition, which achieved nothing except the occupation of Jamaica. Nevertheless, the plan, known as Cromwell's "Western Design," indicates the persistence of the idea that England must expand to the South. This hope led in the years to come to the settlement of the Carolinas and Georgia, and the attempt to make these colonies sources of the products which seventeenth- and eighteenth-century economists believed the English empire must produce to retain its prosperity.

II

Imperial Prosperity from Southern Plantations

IF THE DELUSION of quick riches from the discovery of gold died hard as Englishmen contemplated the resources of America, another dream almost as intoxicating took its place. Indescribable good things might be found in the vegetable and animal kingdoms, and prosperity and plenty would flow from the fields and streams of the New World. Even more exciting to many an Englishman nursing his gout or other ailment was the belief that curative herbs of wondrous potency were to be had overseas for the picking. Since 1577, English readers had been wistfully contemplating a book called *Joyfull Newes Out Of The Newe Founde Worlde,* translated by a merchant named John Frampton from the Spanish of Nicholas Monardes. This volume assured the public that cures for most of the ills of mankind would be forthcoming from America. And that portion of America most productive of desirable products was the southern region. In popular belief the sun-drenched climates were most like paradise and would produce all of the good things which man had possessed before the fall of Adam.

Both California and Florida still employ press agents to keep that doctrine alive.

In the 1560's someone in contact with Spanish America, probably John Hawkins, introduced tobacco, believed to be a strong and beneficent medicine, and its use set in motion a chain reaction which had far-reaching effects on the development of the British Empire. Also introduced soon thereafter were other vegetable products, notably potatoes, both white and sweet, which proved to be valuable supplements to the diet. In addition to their food value, physicians assured potato-eaters that this food had other virtues including the power to stimulate the affections of tender love. The price of potatoes responded accordingly.

Men had once thought of America as a series of gold mines; now they began to talk of the country as one vast herb garden or plantation of good things, especially those vegetables and fruits which grew in tropical climates. Ponce de Leon had believed that Florida would reveal a fountain of youth. More prosaic Anglo-Saxons contented themselves with an array of new herbs, fruits, gums, and drugs which might confer some of the same benefits. The early promotional literature is filled with extravagant descriptions of Nature's abundance in the land to the south.

The bounty of Nature would provide the commodities, said propagandists and pamphleteers, to make England prosperous. The unpeopled land across the seas would also make a place for the surplus population and create a market for more English goods. The English have been called a "nation of shopkeepers"—a nation whose primary interest is business and commerce. We Americans have attained our own commercial civilization by a natural inheritance. This instinct for commerce—as contrasted with the mere search for treasure—is evident from the earliest proposals for English expansion in the New World.

The first book describing Virginia, for example, gives an excellent statement of the mercantilist point of view and follows it with an enumeration of the multitude of merchantable commodities by which Virginia would enrich itself and the mother country. This work, *A briefe and true report of the new found land of Virginia* (1588), by Thomas Hariot, a scientific observer, is worth our attention for the way it emphasized a point of view which dominated English policy for the next two centuries. The first chapter of the book, Hariot promises, "will make declaration of such commodities there alreadie found or to be raised, which will not onely serue the ordinary turnes of you which are and shall bee the planters and inhabitants, but such an ouerplus sufficiently to bee yelded, or by men of skill to bee prouided, as by way of trafficke and exchaunge with our owne nation of England, will enrich your selues the prouiders, those that shal deal with you, the enterprisers in general, and greatly profit our owne countrey men, to supply them with most things which heretofore they haue bene faine to prouide, either of strangers or of our enemies: which commodities for distinction sake, I call Merchantable."[1]

The notion of a self-sufficient closed commercial empire, which would not need to buy from strangers and enemies, was to grow stronger with the passing years. Already Hariot in 1588 thought he had discovered in Virginia (really the coast of what is now North Carolina) a source for some of the exotic commodities which England was to seek, usually in vain, during the next century.

Significantly Hariot begins his chapter of "merchantable" commodities with a discussion of silk, for silk had to be imported from Asia, or bought from Italians, Frenchmen, Portuguese, or Spaniards. In contemporary thinking, its purchase represented a great drain on the economy.

Silk was to be a greater will-o'-the-wisp than gold mines had ever been. From Raleigh's colony to the settlement of Georgia, the imperial economy would demand the production of silk, and always success evaded the planners. Englishmen unhappily had to pay dearly for an extravagant fashion which made courtiers and gentlemen rustle in silk doublets and hose. Even after the eighteenth century had introduced a more subdued fashion in dress for men, satin and taffeta gowns for women consumed an enormous yardage of silk. One has only to look at a few portraits of ladies by Gainsborough, Reynolds, and Romney to realize that even if the world of fashion was small, it took thousands of yards of silk to clothe it. At the time of Oglethorpe's project for settling Georgia, England's annual silk bill averaged approximately £500,000 sterling, and for the preceding century and a half England had been paying huge sums for this fabric.

Hariot thought that Virginia would soon supply silk for home consumption and for commerce. He had observed a silk-fibred grass similar to a type common in Persia "which is in the selfe same climate as Virginia, of which very many of the silke workes that come from thence into Europe are made." He also was hopeful of worm silk, for "in manie of our iourneyes we founde silke wormes fayre and great" and "there is no doubt but if art be added in planting of mulberry trees and others fitte for them in commodious places . . . there will rise as great a profite in time to the Virginians, as thereof doth now to the Persians, Turkes, Italians, and Spaniards."² A warm climate like that of Persia was what Hariot thought he had found in Virginia, and undoubtedly the products which the Levant Company and the East India Company had brought from the East would soon be flowing from the New World.

Among the merchantable commodities which Hariot believed Virginia could produce were many others which England had imported: drugs and rare gums, oils, wine, cedar wood, furs, iron, copper, alum, pitch, tar, rosin, and turpentine. Among the drugs was sassafras, a fragrant shrub used to this day as a folk remedy. Sassafras tea, drunk in April and May, is supposed to cure spring fever. So highly was it prized by the early seventeenth century that many cargoes of sassafras were shipped back to English markets.

Second only to silk in the volume of money required for its purchase was wine. Foreigners from the warmer countries, notably Portugal and Spain, had long profited from English thirst, and English merchants looked forward hopefully to colonies in a climate where grape vines would flourish. Consequently Hariot's observations on the grapes of Virginia stirred new hope: "There are two kinds of grapes that the soile doth yeeld naturally: the one is small and sowre of the ordinarie bignesse as ours in England: the other farre greater & of himselfe lushious sweet. When they are planted and husbanded as they ought, a principall commoditie of wines by them may be raised." The big luscious grapes were muscadines or scuppernongs, and Hariot's words were at least partially prophetic, for though wine-making never succeeded in bolstering the economy of Virginia, home-made scuppernong wine has comforted many a Southerner from that day to this.

The promise of wine production in Virginia impressed other early travellers some of whom were even more enthusiastic than Hariot. William Strachey, for example, writing about 1610, comments that "we have eaten there as full and lushious a grape as in the villages between Paris and Amiens, and I have drunck often of the rathe [early] wine, which Doctor Bohune and other of our people have made full as good, as your French British wyne. Twenty gallons at a time have bene sometimes made without any other helpe then by crushing the grape with the hand, which letting to settle five or six daies, hath in the drawing forth proved strong and headdy. Unto what perfection might not these be brought by the art and industry of manie skillful vineroones [vignerons], being thus naturally good."[3]

Like the desire for silk production, the hope of growing grapes and making wine for commerce persisted for many generations. At the beginning of the eighteenth century Robert Beverley made elaborate attempts to produce wine commercially at his plantation in King and Queen County, Virginia. He was scarcely more successful than others had been. John Fontaine, a French Huguenot, with characteristic French logic, accounted for Beverley's failure by pointing out that he followed Spanish instead of French methods in wine production.[4]

Most of the early writers on English expansion had the mercantilist point of view and realized that the greatest profits eventually would come from the colonial production of raw materials which England had to buy outside of what today we would call the "sterling area." Captain John Smith in 1606 emphasized the commercial possibilities of Virginia: "Muscovia and Polonia [Russia and Poland] doe yearely receive many thousands for pitch, tarre, sope-ashes, Rosen, Flax, Cordage, Sturgeon, Masts, Yards, Wainscot, Firres, Glasses, and such like; also Swethland [Sweden] for Iron and Copper. France in like manner, for wine, Canvas, and Salt. Spaine as much for Iron, Steele, Figges, Reasons [raisins], and Sackes [wine]. Italy with Silkes and Velvets consumes our chiefe Commodities. Holland maintaines it selfe by fishing and trading at our owne doores." Virginia, Smith assured the reader, could provide all of these commodities within the scope of a hundred miles, "either ready provided by nature, or else to be prepared were but industrious men to labour."[5]

The Muscovy Company which imported from the Baltic forests most of the naval stores required by English vessels was at the mercy of the whims of Russia, which was as difficult to deal with in the seventeenth century as it is in the twentieth. One thing our own diplomats ought to know is that Russian behavior is historically consistent, whether the ruler be Ivan the Terrible or Joseph Stalin. If the magnificent forests of Virginia could supply all of the needs of the royal navy and English shipping, that service alone would justify the expense of colonization. For various reasons Virginia's forests did not meet expectations for forest products, but eventually the long leaf pines of South Carolina and Georgia supplied a profitable trade in rosin and turpentine—valuable commodities in international trade to this day.

So important was the colonization of the earthly paradise in Virginia by Englishmen that the endeavor became a patriotic crusade. The Virginia Company enlisted the services of the clergy, a very good substitute in the seventeenth century for the British Broadcasting Company. Preachers extolled the virtues of Virginia in the pulpit and pictured the new country as little short of celestial in its promise. For example, the Reverend Daniel Price, a fashionable London preacher and chaplain to Prince Henry, delivered a sermon on May 28, 1609 which is typical of the clergy's extravagant praise of Virginia. Published by authority of the Virginia Company under the title of *Saul's Prohibition Staide . . . with a reproofe of those that traduce the Honourable Plantation of Virginia. Preached in a Sermon Commaunded at Pauls Crosse* (1609), this sermon condemned to hell all those who libelled Virginia and pictured the new country as "the Barne of Britaine, as Sicily was to Rome, or the Garden of the world as was Thessaly, or the Argosie of the world as is Germany."[6] Virginia, said Price, would soon surpass Persia, Tyre, Babylon, Arabia, Spain, and other countries, ancient and modern, in the supply of spices, silks, dyes, oils, rare woods, and other precious commodities. Moreover, investors in this godly enterprise would have an insurance not vouchsafed other speculators, for God himself would grant them an "vnspeakable blessing" for bringing the message of salvation to the Indians. "You will make . . . A Sauadge country to become a sanctifyed Country; you will obtaine their best commodities; they will obtaine the sauing of their Soules; you will enlarge the boundes of this Kingdome, nay the bounds of heauen."

Here openly asserted with ecclesiastical authority is the statement of profit in the saving of heathen souls for Protestant Christianity with the distinct implication that Virginia is presently to be a corner of heaven itself. English travellers in the nineteenth century were to ridicule Americans for their bumptiousness in declaring that the United States was "God's country," as if it had the special favor of the Deity. That assertion was made in the early seventeenth century by Daniel Price and scores of other pious promoters of English colonization.

The Virginia Company and later the royal authorities under James I and Charles I took steps to see that Virginia became a source of the commodities which were causing the greatest drain of cash into foreign pockets, namely silk and wine. The newly-established House of Burgesses in 1619, on instructions from London, passed a law that every man in Virginia owning land should plant six mulberry trees annually for seven years to nourish silk worms.[7] The mulberry trees flourished all right but the worms suffered from sundry mishaps. Just when it looked as if the infant industry would get a start, rats destroyed the cocoons.

King James himself busied his royal brain with schemes to encourage silk production. Already religious refugees from France and other Continental countries had set up silk-spinning and weaving shops in England and the King hoped to produce the raw silk for this hopeful industry in his new colony of Virginia. To promote this enterprise—and some others almost as important—he instructed one John Bonoeil, a Frenchman in charge of the Royal silk works, to compile a treatise. When the book was done, James himself wrote a preface and the whole thing was published under the title of *His Maiesties Gracious Letter To The Earle of South-Hampton, Treasurer, and to the Councell and Company of Virginia heere: commanding the present setting vp of Silkworkes, and planting of Vines in Virginia. . . . Also a Treatise of the Art of making Silke: Or, Directions for the making of lodgings, and the breeding, nourishing, and ordering of Silkewormes, and for the planting of Mulbery trees, and all other things belonging to the Silke Art. Together with instructions how to plant and dresse Vines, and to make Wine, and how to dry Raisins, Figs, and other fruits, and to set Oliues, Oranges, Lemons, Pomegranates, Almonds, and many other fruits, &c. And in the end, a Conclusion, with sundry profitable remonstrances to the Colonies. Set foorth for the benefit of the two renowned and most hopefull Sisters, Virginia and the Summer-Ilands. By Iohn Boneil Frenchman, seruant in these imployments to his most Excellent Maiesty of Great Brittaine, France, Ireland, Virginia, and the Summer-Ilands. Published by Authority* (1622). With all the weight of the Crown behind it, this treatise ought to have been effective, but like government efforts in the promotion of analogous enterprises in later times, it failed. Recently we have read in the newspapers about British efforts to relieve the shortage of fats at home by raising groundnuts [peanuts] in Africa and the enormous losses incurred, and of the plan to produce poultry and eggs for home consumption on African farms. From King James' time to Mr. Attlee's, the government has had ill-luck in promoting these enterprises of imperial benefit. Ignorance, weather, and pests often confound the dreams of statesmen.

King James' letter prefatory to Bonoeil's treatise is indicative of the seriousness with which the government viewed the necessity of producing silk and wine within the empire. "Whereas We vnderstand that the Soyle in Virginia naturally yeeldeth store of excellent Mulberry trees," wrote the English Solomon, "We haue taken into Our Princely consideration the great benefit that may grow to the Aduenturers and Planters, by the breed of Silkewormes, and setting vp of Silkeworkes in those parts. And therefore of Our gracious Inclination to a designe of so much honour and aduantage to the publike, Wee haue thought good, as at sundry other times, so now more particularly to recommend it to your speciall care, hereby charging and requiring you to take speedy order, that our people there vse all possible diligence in breeding Silkewormes, and erecting Silkeworkes, and that they rather bestow their trauell in compassing this rich and solid Commodity then in Tobacco, which besides much vnnecessary expence, brings with it many disorders and inconueniences. And for as much as Our Seruant, Iohn Bonoeil hath taken paines in setting downe the true vse of the Silkeworme, together with the Art of Silkemaking, and of planting Vines, and that his experience and abilities may much conduce to the aduancement of this business; We doe hereby likewise require you to cause his directions, both for the said Silkeworkes and Vineyards, to bee carefully put in practice thorowout our Plantations there, that so the worke may goe on cheerfully, and receiue no more interruptions nor delayes."

To his royal majesty, it must have seemed simple to decree the production of these commodities which would redress the balance of trade with the rest of the world, but unhappily, about the time Bonoeil's book reached Virginia, the Indians fell on the settlements in the terrible massacre of 1622, a calamity which nearly wiped out the colony. For several years, the Virginians were more concerned about survival than with King James' plans for the empire.

It is worth noting that the King here makes an attack in passing on the production of tobacco, a commodity which he had condemned the year after he ascended the throne in *A Counter Blaste To Tobacco* (1604). Having gone on record as opposed to the use of tobacco, the King felt obliged to continue his hostility. Already, however, signs indicated that tobacco might prove the most profitable crop produced in Virginia.

About 1612, John Rolfe began to experiment with the growing of tobacco. Within four years it had become a staple crop and was planted even in the streets and marketplace of Jamestown. The use of tobacco had already taken such a firm hold on Englishmen that in 1614 it was estimated that England's annual tobacco bill amounted to £200,000 sterling and someone complained in Parliament that even preachers smelled of smoke and poor men each night spent a large portion of their daily wages on pipe tobacco.[8] Even though King James might not approve, it was clear that here was a product which would have to be produced within the empire or else the drain on the economy would be almost as great as that for silk and wine.

Some tobacco was produced in England, but before Rolfe's experiments most of it had come from Spain, to the distress of English imperialists. In 1620 one Edward Bennett published *A Treatise deuided into three parts touching the inconueniences that the Importation of Tobacco out of Spaine hath brought into this Land.* Using some of the same arguments made by the advocates of silk culture, Bennett urged the production of tobacco within the empire. "The maine decay of Trade," he pointed out, "and the chiefe cause that hindreth the importation of Bullion out of Spaine is Tobacco, for there is consumed by all computation, yearely in this Land, three hundred thousand weight."[9] The Spanish tobacco trade, Bennett argues, has hindered the development of Virginia and the Bermudas. The encouragement of tobacco production in these colonies, he asserts, would create prosperity and establish a strong bulwark against

Spain. Incidentally, Bennett insisted that the Spaniards were very uncleanly in the way they handled their tobacco. He is probably the first to use a theme which tobacco advertisers in a later time appear to have found effective.

The popularity of tobacco and its potentialities for the trade of England had not been anticipated by the economic planners who were slow to realize that at last a luxury product had been discovered which could be produced within the frame of empire. Once that fact was demonstrated, the government took steps to see that England reaped the maximum benefits from the tobacco trade. Government regulations from the time of James I onward forbade the growing of tobacco in England itself and decreed that tobacco grown in the colonies should be shipped directly to English ports for processing. Thus the government reaped a substantial revenue from duties and brought in a product in great demand in the foreign trade. The sale of tobacco abroad, even in competition with Spanish and Dutch tobacco, helped to offset the unfavorable cash position created by purchases of non-empire products like silk and wine.

The production of tobacco, which had come into English trade almost by the backdoor, occupied a place of first importance in the imperial economy in the later seventeenth and eighteenth centuries. So profitable was the trade that many merchants of London and Bristol devoted themselves exclusively to it, and the production of tobacco was the main concern of planters in Virginia, Maryland, and in a portion of the Carolinas. Such a concentration was not without its penalties because a crop failure, or a glut of the market by overproduction, might cause a widespread financial disaster. Wise leaders in the colonies argued earnestly against the hazards of the one crop system, a system which has often been the ruin of the South, but profits were large in good years, and the pressures were great, both at home and abroad, to raise more and more tobacco. When the Reverend James Blair at the end of the seventeenth century was arguing with the Board of Trade that they should help establish a college to save the souls of Virginians, Sir Edward Seymour, a Lord of the Treasury, exclaimed, "Souls! Damn your souls? Make tobacco!"[10] To the empire builders, tobacco was more important even than salvation, and they prized the tobacco colonies on the Chesapeake above those sometimes recalcitrant and always competitive offspring to the north.

Tobacco was an ideal commodity from the point of view of the seventeenth- and eighteenth-century mercantilists. It was produced in the raw state in the colonies; it was shipped from the colonies to the mother country, paying an export tax in the colony and an import tax at home; and it could be processed in England to become a lucrative article of export. Furthermore it could be raised with unskilled labor, such labor as could be supplied by African slaves, themselves an article of profitable commerce to the Royal African Company. The usefulness of the rawest slaves from the west coast of Africa in the tobacco fields of Virginia, Maryland, and Bermuda helped to fasten a system of labor and a racial problem upon the Southern colonies which had evil consequences persisting to our own day.

Although the very success of tobacco as a money crop was a hindrance to the production of other desired commodities, the planners did not abandon hope that Virginia would eventually compete with France, Spain, Italy, Persia, and the East Indies in exotic products. The distribution of John Bonoeil's treatise in 1622 was accompanied by orders from the Virginia Company commanding efforts to produce silk and wine. Skilled artisans from Southern Europe came to Virginia to instruct the settlers in these crafts, and experimentation led some Virginians to believe as late as 1649 that silk and wine would supersede in time tobacco in popular favor, but their optimism was ill-founded. The profits from sugar in Barbados induced a few planters to try to plant sugar cane, but nothing came of this. The grapes, lemons, oranges, ginger, and figs, recommended to the planters, likewise failed, and tobacco ruled supreme. In 1705 Robert Beverley the historian complained that Virginians were so entrapped in the one crop system and so lacking in enterprise that they would not even use their abundant timber for making their own wooden ware but instead imported it from England. By this time, however, the Board of Trade in London had come to approve of Virginia and Maryland's complete concentration upon tobacco, which fitted well with mercantile theory. They would try elsewhere to produce the other desired materials.

One of the commodities which international trade in the Elizabethan period had popularized, and which England now wanted to produce, was sugar. Sugar like silk was a product which cost England cash, cash which went to Italian, Spanish, and Portuguese producers. In early times, Englishmen had depended on the bees to provide their sweets, and many ancient recipes specified honey for sweetening. But in the sixteenth century, trade with the Canary and Madeira Islands brought sugar into fairly common use. By the early seventeenth century it was an essential.

Sugar was believed to have great curative values and to be a preservative of health. John Gerard, the herbalist, asserted that "It drieth and cleanseth the stomacke, maketh smooth the roughness of the breast and lungs, cleareth the voice, and putteth away hoarsenesse, the cough, and all sournesse and bitternesse."[11] And a seventeenth century physician had a saying that

"If Sugar can preserve both Pears and Plumbs,

Why can it not preserve as well our Lungs?"[12]

Even if sugar had not possessed these healing virtues, it was pleasant to the taste and Englishmen even used it to qualify their drinks. But England was not a sugar-producing nation, and the government was troubled.

Sugar canes had been taken from the Canaries to Brazil and had flourished. From Brazil, sugar cane had spread to the Spanish islands of the West Indies. Perhaps Englishmen might find a place where they too could produce sugar. About 1640 conditions on Barbados forced the planters there to think of a crop to take the place of tobacco. Stimulated by the demand for tobacco on the European market, the Barbadians had raised more of the weed than they could sell. Faced with bankruptcy because of the glut of the tobacco market, they were ready to try anything and sugar cane looked promising. The cane grew so luxuriantly on Barbados that within a short time sugar had superseded tobacco as the principal industry on that island, and it quickly spread to other British territory in the Caribbean.

On the mainland of North America English planters had no success with sugar cane in the colonial period. But Barbados became a sugar paradise. Since sugar making required expensive equipment, only those planters with large capital could operate the plantations and refineries. Consequently many of the smaller planters, who had done well with tobacco, had to leave Barbados in search of greener pastures. Many of them came to South Carolina and helped to establish the economy of that colony on a sound basis, as we shall see later.

The sugar making of Barbados was so profitable in imperial trade that by 1675 over four hundred vessels were engaged in the transport of sugar and molasses.[13] A by-product of molasses, rum, became a national drink and another commodity enormously important in international commerce. The sugar islands were so prized by the mother country that when the Peace of Paris in 1763 ended the Seven Years War, some English politicians wanted to allow France to retain Canada on condition that she cede the French islands in the West Indies to Great Britain.

These French West Indian possessions had proved so enormously valuable as sources of sugar and molasses that English merchants were anxious to obtain them. The demand for rum had long outstripped the capacity of Barbados and the other British islands to supply the necessary raw material, namely molasses, but nevertheless England tried to prevent the colonies from developing an independent trade with the French West Indies. As early as 1733, England passed the first Molasses Act to restrict the trade to the British possessions and succeeded only in stimulating wholesale smuggling between the French islands and New England, where the manufacture of rum had become an important factor in the Northern colonies' prosperity. This disrespect for imperial regulations by the Northern colonies was one more reason why the home government found the Southern colonies more to their liking.

By the middle of the seventeenth century, England had succeeded in developing two profitable tropical products within the empire, namely tobacco and sugar. The cash which these commodities brought into England confirmed still further the belief held by many of the mercantile imperialists that the most desirable colonies would be those established in the South. Pleased with the profits from tobacco and sugar, Englishmen for the next century continued their endeavor to find a modern counterpart of the Garden of Eden in the warmer parts of America where they might yet produce all of those exotic commodities which had previously defied the best efforts of their statesmen.

III

Eden and Utopia
South of Virginia

THE NOTION THAT the earthly paradise, similar to if
not the veritable site of the Scriptural Eden, might be
found in some southern region of the New World was
widely held in the seventeenth and early eighteenth
centuries. Explorers from Virginia expected to find the
Great South Sea somewhere to the southwest and they
believed its shores would be a land like Eden. In the
summer of 1650, Edward Bland, an English merchant
resident in Virginia, and Abraham Wood, a militia
captain and Indian trader, led an expedition from the
site of Petersburg to a point in southwest Virginia where
they discovered a river which they believed ran west
into the South Sea.[1] The next year Bland printed in
London *The Discovery of New Britain* (1651), which
carried a preface extolling the land and urging all who
desired "the advancement of God's glory by the con-
version of the Indians [and] the augmentation of the
English commonwealth in extending its liberties" to
consider "the present benefit and future profits" of settling the new territory lying between thirty-five and
thirty-seven degrees of north latitude.

This geographical position carried a mystical signifi-
cance. Bland's book reprinted a passage attributed to
Sir Walter Raleigh's *Marrow of History,* pointing out
that God had placed Eden on the thirty-fifth parallel of
north latitude.[2] This location guaranteed an ideal climate of perpetual spring and summer, a garden shaded
by palm trees, described by Raleigh as the greatest blessing and wonder of nature. Other earthly paradises, the
passage implied, would be found along the thirty-fifth
parallel, presumably also shaded by palm trees and producing dates, raisins, spices, and everything else which
Adam had had for his comfort. This location would put
paradise along a line connecting Newbern and Fayette-
ville, North Carolina, with Chattanooga and Memphis,
Tennessee.

When Lieutenant Governor Alexander Spotswood of
Virginia in 1716 led an exploring expedition across the
Blue Ridge Mountains, he discovered a river which we
now call the Shenandoah but which Spotswood and his
company named the Euphrates, after one of the four
rivers of Eden, because the country looked to them like
paradise. The explanation of why this spot appeared
so rosy at that time may be found, however, in an account
of the expedition, which must have been one of the
most convivial on record. On the very crest of the ridge,
the explorers stopped to drink the health of King George
I, and the opportunity seemed appropriate to celebrate
still further. "We had a good dinner," reported John
Fontaine, chronicler of the expedition, "and after it we
got the men together, and loaded all their arms, and we
drank the King's health in champagne, and fired a vol-

ley; the Princess' health in burgundy, and fired a volley; and all the rest of the royal family in claret, and fired a volley. We drank the Governor's health and fired another volley: We had several sorts of liquor, viz., Virginia red wine and white wine, Irish usquebaugh, brandy, shrub, two sorts of rum, champagne, canary, cherry punch, water, cider, etc."[33] After these potations, the driest river bed in Arizona, much less the Valley of Virginia, would have seemed a land flowing with milk and honey.

When William Byrd II of Westover, Virginia, set out to promote the sale of a large tract of land which he had acquired on the Dan River near the border between North Carolina and Virginia, he called his property the Land of Eden and supplied notes to a German-Swiss land agent named Jenner who published in Switzerland in 1737 an alluring promotional tract under the title of *Neu-gefundenes Eden* [New Found Eden]. The description of Byrd's property was intended to leave no doubt in the reader's mind that here indeed was the earthly paradise.

Because promoters had lately been recommending South Carolina and Georgia to hopeful Swiss emigrants as lands of fertility and felicity, Byrd's agent goes to some pains to prove that this particular Eden far surpasses any other. "I am pleased to have the opportunity to make it known to my fellow countrymen, the Swiss," Jenner remarks with an air of objectivity, "that they [may] turn their thoughts to this beautiful, healthful and fertile land, and renounce miserable and unhealthful South Carolina, since [there] they will find after all

nothing but poverty, sickness, and early death . . ."
South Carolina, Jenner argues, is trying to create a fortress on its southern border, or Georgia, and wants settlers in that unwholesome spot. And he cites what he
says is an English proverb, "Whoever desires to die soon,
just go to Carolina."[4]

The exact reverse is Byrd's Land of Eden. There the
climate is perfect, the air is pure, the water is as sweet
as milk, and the sun shines every day of the year. When
it rains, it rains gently at night sufficient to keep the
heavenly place well-watered. In this mild and beneficent
land, disease is practically unknown and Europeans who
come ailing soon find themselves restored to health, and
"what is much more miraculous, the old people receive
quite new strength, feel as if they were wholly born anew,
that is, much stronger, much more light-footed, and in
every way much more comfortable than before . . ."[5]

The products of this Eden, we will not be surprised
to learn, are practically all those which a settler—or the
British Board of Trade—might desire. At last, in the
Dan River bottoms, if one believes this tract, the production of silk and wine is assured, along with other good
things. "One could make silk also very easily," the author
asserts, "because the land is full of mulberry trees, and
requires little exertion. People have already tried this,
and obtained very beautiful silk. The English, however,
do not want to go to any trouble in this. Cotton grows
in sufficiency in this land. One can merely pick it and
spin it, and make all kinds of materials from it for use.
It is also a very good ware in trade." Flax, hemp, indigo,
grains, fruits, and herbs of all descriptions flourish.

Grapes grow in great abundance and have already proved
their utility and "therefore nothing is lacking but good
grape people."⁶ Especially valuable is the sugar maple
tree: "This is the most useful tree in the whole world,
because one makes wine, spirits, vinegar, honey, and
sugar from it, which comes from its juice."⁷ Verily
nothing was lacking in Eden but a happy people to con-
sume its products. Unfortunately the ship loaded with
the Swiss emigrants who heeded the siren words of the
promoter wrecked off the coast of North Carolina and
only a handful survived to reach the promised land. For
all the fine promises, William Byrd never succeeded in
turning the rich bottom lands along the Dan River into
the paradise his agent pictured. To this day the land
is reasonably fertile but its products have always been
such prosaic things as corn, cotton, and tobacco.

Notwithstanding William Byrd's low opinion of South
Carolina, as indicated in the *New Found Eden,* and an
equally low opinion of North Carolina, which he had
expressed in *The History of the Dividing Line,* the
Carolinas proved highly profitable to the empire and
won the approval of merchants, bankers, and politicians
in London. Although their products were not precisely
the ones which the mercantilists had originally intended,
they fulfilled perfectly the current idea of the proper
relation between colony and mother country. Even that
irascible and hard-to-please agent of the Crown, Edward
Randolph, surveyor-general of His Majesty's Customs
for North America, had only words of praise in a report
which he made to the Board of Trade in London on
March 16, 1699. "The great improvement made in this

Province is wholly owing to the industry and labour of the Inhabitants," he wrote. "They have applied themselves to make such commodities as might increase the revenue of the Crown, as Cotton, Wool, Ginger, Indigo, etc. But finding them not to answer the end, they are set upon making Pitch, Tar, and Turpentine, and planting of rice, and can send over great quantityes yearly, if they had encouragement from England, . . ."[8]

The Carolinas, Randolph reported, are a much better source for naval stores than New England: "My Lords, I did formerly present Your Lordships with proposals for supplying England with Pitch and Tar, Masts and all our Naval Stores from New England. . . . But since my arrival here I find I am come into the only place for such commodities upon the Continent of America."[9] By this statement he meant the *best* place, not literally the only place. The value of the tar, pitch, masts, and other supplies helped to bring prosperity to the Carolinas and security to the Royal Navy.

In other ways the Carolinas, especially South Carolina, pleased the mercantilists. A constant stream of raw materials poured out of Charleston and into English channels of industry and commerce. For instance, South Carolina developed a great trade in deerskins needed by the leathermakers and glovers. Furs from the backcountry also added to the revenue. Unlike the Chesapeake Bay colonies, which depended upon tobacco for their money crop, the Southeast developed a diverse commerce centered in Charleston, and of this commerce, the deerskin and fur trade contributed much to colonial and imperial prosperity.

So much attention has been lavished on the fur trade of other regions that we forget the importance of the South in this connection. Louisiana is still the largest fur-producing region in North America. Throughout the eighteenth century Charleston, South Carolina, was the great skin and fur market. Some of the toughest characters in all North America brought their pack trains of deerskins and furs to Charleston each spring. The tinkle of the packhorse bells and the clatter of hoofs on the cobble stones of the Battery brought Charlestonians to their windows to view picturesque traders, some well-known and famous as Indian fighters.

The caravans often brought long strings of Indian captives to be sold as slaves to Barbados and other islands of the West Indies. We must also remember this dark chapter in the history of commerce. Charleston was an important slaving port. Captured Indians by the hundreds were sold to ship captains headed for the West Indies, and Negroes by the thousands were brought into Charleston from Africa. Indian slaves were not dependable in the Carolinas, for they might escape to the forests and make their way back to their tribes, but African Negroes had no such hope. They proved useful laborers in the pine forests and hot fields of the coastal plain. The traffic in slaves and the commodities which they produced made rich the merchants and shipowners of London and Bristol as well as their agents in Charleston.

South Carolina gave promise late in the seventeenth century of becoming the dream colony of the English mercantilists. Some of the inhabitants wrote to London in the year 1691 that "We are encouraged with severall new rich Comodityes as Silck, Cotton, Rice and Indigo, which are naturally produced here."[10]   Silk remained a delusion, but rice, indigo, and eventually cotton became indeed "rich commodities."   The first of these to be grown extensively was rice, which flourished in the alluvial swamp lands of the coastal region.   Although colonists even in Virginia had experimented with rice, not until the last decade of the seventeenth century, in South Carolina, was it grown extensively.   The legend that a shipmaster from Madagascar, accidentally touching at Charleston in 1696, left a half-bushel of rice seed from which grew the Carolina rice industry, is apparently only a half-truth,[11] but from that date until the mid-nineteenth century rice was an increasingly important article of commerce with England.

To an extraordinary woman, Eliza Lucas, South Carolina owed the development of the production of indigo, a vegetable dye much in demand in the eighteenth century when clothing of this hue was especially fashionable. In the year 1739, Eliza Lucas, then just sixteen, found herself established as manager of a plantation on the west side of the Ashley River above Charleston. Her father, Lieutenant Colonel George Lucas, was stationed at Antigua in the West Indies, but since his wife was sickly and could not endure that climate, he moved his family to South Carolina and put this remarkable girl in charge of the family plantation. In a letter to her father written in July 1739, she reported that she was trying "to bring the Indigo, Ginger, Cotton, and Lucern and Casada [cassava] to perfection and had greater hopes from the Indigo (if I could have the seed earlier next year from the West Indies) than of ye rest of ye things I had try'd."[12] After many discouragements, not only in raising the plants, but in producing the dye, Eliza achieved success. By 1747-48, the production was such that the port of Charleston exported 138,334 pounds of the dyestuff. When the British government offered a bounty in 1748 for the production of the dye in the British-American colonies, some growers found it so profitable that they doubled their capital every three or four years.[13]

The production of indigo within the empire was important, for the source of most of the dye would otherwise have been the French West Indies. Since England was at war with France through a good part of the eighteenth century, it was imperative that she not buy this useful commodity from the enemy. The power of fashion was such, however, that the clothiers and dyers would have obtained the dye even if they had been obliged to deal in the enemy's black market. The solution of course was to stimulate production in the tropical and semitropical areas of the British dominions, an operation which proved highly successful.

The production of cotton, another article which England had bought outside the empire, was less successful than indigo and rice, but some cotton was produced in the various Southern colonies and in the West Indies in the period before the Revolution. Few of us stop to realize the importance of cotton in the social progress of mankind. The importation into England of cheap cotton textiles from India, brought about by the expansion of the East India Company's activities in the seventeenth century, for the first time made it possible for Englishmen of average means to be reasonably clean. Up to that time linen was the only available fabric for undergarments, and linen, then as now, was expensive.[14]

The East India Company brought in chintzes, muslins, calicoes, and other fabrics. The word calico comes from the name of an Indian town, Calicut. Though the importation of cotton from India gave English merchants an article of trade much in demand on the continent of Europe, the East India Company had to pay out cash for its textiles. If raw cotton could be produced within the empire and woven at home, this would be an advantage to both the industry and commerce of Great Britain.

Although efforts continued throughout the colonial period to stimulate the production of raw cotton, only small amounts reached the markets. In the year 1768, Virginia led the South by exporting 43,350 pounds of ginned cotton. In the same year South Carolina exported only 3,000 pounds, and Georgia, only 300 pounds.[15] During most of the period, planters lacked confidence in the stability of cotton prices—an old complaint—and they found other crops more profitable. The separation of the lint from the seed was also a troublesome problem. Although roller gins were known and used in the colonial period, not until Eli Whitney invented the saw gin in the last decade of the eighteenth century was this problem solved.

By the end of the century South Carolina and Georgia were producing several million pounds of cotton. Although the colonies were now politically free of Great

Britain, trade retained many of its old characteristics. The South continued to supply raw materials for English industry; and of these raw materials, cotton rapidly increased in importance. By the mid-nineteenth century, cotton spinning and weaving had become one of Great Britain's most valuable industries, and raw cotton from the plantations of the Southern states was an essential of international trade. By a curious irony of history, cotton textiles of English manufacture in the nineteenth century ruined the native weaving industry of India, which had first supplied cottons to Britain. And by another reversal of the process, the cheap labor in the Indian cotton mills in the twentieth century ruined the English textile industry by destroying its Asiatic market for cotton goods.

Paralleling the British emphasis on trade in the eighteenth century was a growing spirit of humanitarianism. As in the United States in the twentieth century, the brotherhood of man and the acquisition of material property were somehow equated. As humanitarians and mercantilists, often one and the same, viewed the southern American colonies, they warmed with enthusiasm over the prospect of discovering there at last the perfect paradise where all men could be happy and prosperous as they produced the commodities which served the best interests of the British Empire. Occasionally the humanitarians contemplated the institution of slavery, which seemed to be necessary for prosperity, and found it disturbing; but usually they salved their consciences by thinking of the boon of Christianity which slavery had brought to the heathen whom they imported from Africa.

George Whitefield, the evangelist, for example, wept over man's sins and distress, but he recommended slavery for Georgia and helped pay the expenses of Bethesda, his orphan home, from the profits of a South Carolina plantation worked with slaves.

As the humanitarian planners contemplated the opportunities in the South, they had visions of new Edens in which the poor and oppressed of England would find a refuge; there the erstwhile indigents would work out their salvation and keep a steady stream of profitable raw materials pouring into the home ports. Some of the planners had read More's *Utopia,* Bacon's essay "Of Plantations," James Harrington's *The Commonwealth of Oceana* (1656), or some other treatise on ideal commonwealths. The spirit of social experiment was in the air. Furthermore the atmosphere was also heavily charged with the excitement of speculation. During 1719 and the early part of 1720, men and women rushed to buy stock in the South Sea Company which doubled, trebled, quadrupled and further multiplied in value as they watched it. Before the bubble burst in August 1720, other speculations promised similar incredible profits. It was an age of "projectors," or promoters, some of whom picked the region embracing this very spot as the scene of their activities. No scheme seemed impossible, not even Swift's satirical project to extract sunbeams from cucumbers.

For reasons not difficult to comprehend, the hope of finding a fruitful land in the South appealed strongly to Scots. No country could have been more unlike the hills of Scotland than the coastal plains and river bottoms of the Carolinas and Georgia. Perhaps that was its greatest attraction. During the eighteenth century Scots were among the most important immigrant groups received in the Southern colonies. Because we usually think of the Scots as a practical and thrifty people, convinced that destiny has already settled the affairs of man in accordance with the theology of John Calvin, it may be a surprise to find that some of the most fantastic of the Utopian projects were dreamed up by Scots.

One of the better known and most colorful schemes was hatched in the mind of a Scottish baronet, Sir Robert Montgomery of Skelmorly, who in 1717 published *A Discourse Concerning the design'd Establishment Of a New Colony To The South of Carolina, In The Most delightful Country of the Universe.* This was a plan to establish a colony in the country embraced between the mouths of the Savannah and Altamaha rivers and extending westward to the Great South Sea [the Pacific Ocean]. That included most of the present state of Alabama, not to mention the states westward to the California coast.

Sir Robert described this country, which he named Azilia, as "our future Eden," and he further declared that English writers "universally agree that Carolina, and especially in its Southern Bounds, is the most amiable Country in the Universe: that Nature has not bless'd the World with any Tract, which can be preferable to it, that Paradise, with all her Virgin Beauties, may be modestly suppos'd at most but equal to its Native Excellencies."[16] This territory which exceeded Paradise itself in excellence was claimed by South Carolina, but the Lords Proprietors were more than glad to encourage

Scottish settlers who would serve as a protection against the Spaniards in Florida and the French in Louisiana. Accordingly they granted permission to Sir Robert and his colleagues to settle Azilia.

In a literary genre characterized by optimism, Sir Robert Montgomery's *Discourse* is surely one of the most hopeful ever printed. Azilia, as he describes it, "lies in the same Latitude with Palestine Herself, That promis'd Canaan, which was pointed out by God's own Choice, to bless the Labours of a favourite People. It abounds with Rivers, Woods, and Meadows. Its gentle Hills are full of Mines, Lead, Copper, Iron, and even some of Silver. 'Tis beautified with odiferous Plants, green all the Year. . . . The Air is healthy, and the Soil in general fruitful, and of infinite Variety; Vines, naturally flourishing upon the Hills, bear Grapes in most luxuriant Plenty. They have every Growth which we possess in England, and almost every Thing that England wants besides. The Orange and the Limon thrive in the same common Orchard with the Apple, and the Pear-Tree, Plumbs, Peaches, Apricots, and Nectarins bear from Stones in three years growing. The Planters raise large Orchards of these Fruits to feed their Hogs with."[17] To Scots and Englishmen, who knew oranges from Seville and lemons from Portugal merely as symbols of luxury, this country, in the same latitude as Palestine, must have appeared indeed as a new Canaan.

To help him in the colonization of Azilia, Montgomery had as associates Aaron Hill, a theatrical poet who claimed to have an invention for making potash, and Amos Kettleby, merchant and politician of London, whom the South Carolina Assembly had dismissed in the previous year from his post as colonial agent. Montgomery was to have the title of Margrave, with a great palace at the exact center of the district where he would reside. There he would live in splendor and rule over a feudal principality peopled with a hierarchy of gentry, tenants, and slaves. Aaron Hill and Amos Kettleby appear to have been more concerned with the financial returns from the venture than with the glories of title.

The chapter in Montgomery's tract headed "Of some Designs in View for making Profit" assures the reader that at long last imperial and mercantilist ambitions are about to be realized in Azilia. "Our Prospects in this Point are more extensive than we think it needful to discover," Montgomery remarks with an air of mystery. "It were a shame shou'd we confine the Fruitfulness of such a rich and lovely Country to some single Product, which Example first makes common, and the being common robs of Benefit. Thus Sugar in Barbadoes, Rice in Carolina, and Tobacco in Virginia take up all the Labours of their People, overstock the Markets, stifle the Demand, and make their Industry their Ruin, . . ." Azilia, however, will not be a one-crop country. Instead it will produce the very commodities which England still has had to buy from foreigners. Montgomery makes this explicit: "Coffee, Tea, Figs, Raisins, Currants, Almonds, Olives, Silk, Wine, Cochineal, and a great Variety of still more rich Commodities which we are forc'd to buy at mighty Rates from Countries lying in the very Latitude of our Plantations: All these we certainly shall Propagate, . . . mean while we shall confine our first

Endeavours to such easy Benefits as will (without the smallest waiting for the Growth of Plants) be offer'd to our Industry from the spontaneous Wealth which overruns the Country."[18] With Aaron Hill's alleged invention in mind, Montgomery promises that potash will be a source of immediate profit.

The happy Margravate of Azilia, alas, was doomed to be a delusion. To transport colonists, to clear land, to build a palace, and even to make potash required capital. There were also political complications. Discouraged at frustrations and delays, Sir Robert Montgomery sold his interest late in 1718 to Aaron Hill the poet. But after the failure of the South Sea Company in 1720, not even Aaron Hill's literary style was sufficiently purple to lure investors in Azilia, and the scheme collapsed. Yet such was the hopefulness of the projectors that one of them, possibly Hill, published two further pamphlets late in 1720, one of which was entitled *A Description of the Golden Islands, with an Account of the Undertaking Now on Foot for Making a Settlement There.* This tract outlined a plan for making a paradise of the sea islands along the coast of Georgia and producing there not only silk and almonds, but "many more Fruits and Drugs, growing in Persia, in India about Lahore, in China, and in Japan.[19] But the public had its fingers too thoroughly burned on the South Sea Company stock to take an interest in the Golden Islands. The Azilian project is worth detailed consideration, however, because it epitomizes the search for Eden which had obsessed British thinking since the beginning of the colonial effort and which was to continue to the end.

Another Scottish baronet, Sir Alexander Cuming of Coulter, even more erratic than Sir Robert Montgomery, conceived a project to settle three hundred thousand Jews on the Cherokee tribal lands in the backcountry of South Carolina. This proposal for a Zion on the Carolina frontier had as its object the relief of oppressed Jewish families in Europe by taking them out of crowded ghettos and establishing them on the land where they could turn their talents and industry to farming and the production of commodities useful to the British Empire. If the government would underwrite the enterprise, Sir Alexander promised, it would presently be able to retire a large portion of the national debt from the profits.

Sir Alexander attributed his zeal for colonial affairs to a vision of his wife's which suggested that he make a journey to the backcountry of South Carolina. Considering the Scot's peculiarities, we cannot escape the suspicion that his wife's vision was a clever ruse to procure a little peace at home. But whatever the motive, Sir Alexander set out in 1729 on a self-appointed mission to Carolina and the Cherokees. Surely the Scottish baronet had read books similar to those which had sent Cervantes' good knight of La Mancha on his adventures, for his travels read like a chapter from *Don Quixote*. Leaving Charleston on March 13, 1730, Sir Alexander travelled during the following month nearly a thousand miles through the Cherokee tribes. Armed to the teeth and boasting of the power and brilliance of his King, George II, the baronet astonished his Indian hearers and persuaded them that he was a great chief representing a king whose power reached even to the hills of South

Carolina. At a tribal council he persuaded the chiefs to kneel and swear allegiance to King George—or so he thought—and he had himself acclaimed the King's viceroy. So persuasive was Sir Alexander's eloquence that he induced six Cherokees, a minor chief and five warriors, to set out with him for London and the King's court. Near Charleston they picked up another stray Indian. When they all reached England, the chief was a king and the other Indians were described as generals or chiefs. On June 18, 1730, King George received the Scot and his Indian protegés. During the next three months the Cherokee "king" and his fellow "chiefs" were the sensation of London. They were entertained, feted, and taught English vices. On September 28, the play of *Orinoco* was performed in their honor at Lincoln's Inn Fields, and so great was the public excitement over the Indians that the theatre's box office receipts trebled that night. When they returned to their tribesmen, the Indians' report of the glories of the English nation probably helped to keep the Cherokees loyal to England in the succeeding wars with France.[20]

Fantastic as were Sir Alexander Cuming's schemes for Cherokee-Jewish Utopias in the foothills of Carolina, the publicity which they received helped to focus further interest on the Southern colonies. The settlement of Georgia itself was a manifestation of the freshly aroused humanitarian, mercantilist, and imperialistic interest in expansion south of the Carolina settlements.

During the summer of 1730, about the time the Cherokees were exciting the London populace, General James Oglethorpe and some of his friends were petition-

ing the King to make them a grant of land south of the
Carolina border "for settling poor persons of London."[21]
The plan, as every school child knows, was prompted by
a desire on the part of this philanthropic group to provide relief for imprisoned debtors. It received favorable
consideration from the government for other reasons.
The need for a bulwark against Spain and France from
the south and southwest was greater than ever. And once
more the merchants and bankers of London were dream-
ing of a source for those raw materials which they still
found it necessary to buy from their enemies. Moved
by so many worthy reasons, the King granted a charter
to Oglethorpe and his fellow trustees on June 9, 1732.
This time a Utopian scheme was to succeed, but not
precisely as Oglethorpe or the government planned it.
For few debtors ever came to Georgia and once more
the vision of exotic produce was a mirage. Nevertheless
Georgia did become a useful colony and an element in
the imperial organization.

The Trustees tried earnestly to make Georgia the
combination of Eden and Utopia which they had en-
visioned. They opened the country to oppressed folk
not only of England but of the Continent as well. They
passed regulations aimed at keeping the commonwealth
pure by excluding rum and forbidding slavery. And they
were determined to produce silk, wine, olives, and other
good things which had always eluded Englishmen. A
poet writing in the *South Carolina Gazette* in 1733 pictured the new colony as a garden of Hesperides. Its silks
would clothe England's beauties; its wine would flow un-
stinted, "refreshing Labour and dispelling Woe"; and

its orchards and groves would be fruitful with dates, lemons, oranges, citrons, limes, almonds, tea and coffee.[21] The trustees included some hard-headed business men who knew such beneficence would not be spontaneous, even in Paradise, in the rational eighteenth century. They therefore encouraged Swiss and other Continental silk-workers to come to Georgia; they ordered every recipient of a grant of land to plant mulberry trees; and they encouraged experimentation with other exotic commodities. But it was all to no avail. Georgia followed South Carolina in depending upon rice, the skin and fur trade, and upon naval stores for the basis of its economy.

The search for an exotic Eden did not end with the settlement of Georgia. The ink on the Treaty of Paris was hardly dry in 1763 before Archibald Menzies of Megerny Castle, Perthshire, devised a plan to people Florida with Armenians, Greeks, and Minorcans, who would be expert in growing olives, grapes, and silk worms. Nothing came of his proposal but four years later a brother Scot, Dr. Andrew Turnbull, and two English associates, Sir William Duncan and Sir Richard Temple, formed a partnership to settle other Greeks, Italians, and Minorcans in Florida. They succeeded actually in establishing a group at New Smyrna on the coast below St. Augustine, but quarreling and fighting among the settlers quickly ruined the enterprises in which the promoters had pinned such hope. When a Scot takes leave of practical matters and begins to spin ingenious plans, the extent of his fantasy is illimitable.

The faith in a Southern Utopia persisted and manifested itself in numerous projects throughout the colonial period and afterward. Time will not permit even the mention of various schemes to create a paradise in the lands south of Virginia. Perhaps the most visionary of all was a project of a sentimental and mystical German from Saxony, one Christian Gottlieb Priber, who devised a plan for a Utopia among the Cherokees on the headwaters of the Tennessee River. A precursor of Rousseau, Priber's state represented a fusion of ideas from Plato's *Republic,* current doctrines of humanitarianism, and concepts of the noble savage which had cropped up from time to time. His efforts to found a communistic state among the Cherokees and to teach them to resist the inroads of the whites and the knavery of traders aroused the antagonism of Georgians who succeeded in arresting Priber in 1743. He was kept a political prisoner and died at Frederica on St. Simon's Island a few years later. Among his manuscripts was one describing his projected Utopian state as the "Kingdom of Paradise." In the opinion of his captors it was "extremely wicked" because "he enumerates many whimsical privileges and natural rights, as he calls them, which his citizens are to be entitled to, particularly dissolving marriages and allowing community of women, and all kinds of licentiousness."[22] His greatest sin, however, lay in his success in winning the friendship of the Indians and developing an organization which threatened the expansion of the British.

The British Empire profited immensely from the Southern colonies, but the mercantilists never succeeded in making these colonies the source of all the exotic commodities they yearned to produce within the empire. The economic planners, then as now, never grasped all of the factors involved in their schemes. For example, they never realized that silk production required both skilled and cheap labor, which the colonies always lacked, a lack which indeed has always been a serious problem in the New World.

The dream of making the South the source of many of the luxuries which mankind requires has never died. In modern times we have seen a certain realization of these hopes in the expansion of the textile industry. If we do not produce worm silk in the South, we at least have manufactories of rayon, nylon, and other chemical substitutes. A Japanese economist was in my office recently lamenting the shift in fashion and production, which had ruined the silk industry of Japan.

Not far from where Swiss and Italian colonists in the eighteenth century sought to establish new industries on the upper Savannah River the United States government is today building a great plant to transform hydrogen into energy. The end product of that effort is yet unknown. Some believe that ultimately the release of energy from such an abundant source will solve most of the problems of mankind. Others, more gloomy, see in it the destruction of civilization. But we are witnessing one more effort to establish Utopia, even at the risk of universal destruction.

Notes

CHAPTER I

1. This subject is treated in more detail in Louis B. Wright, *Religion and Empire: The Alliance between Piety and Commerce in English Expansion, 1558-1625* (Chapel Hill, N. C., 1943), pp. 33-56.
2. Louis B. Wright, "Henry Robarts: Patriotic Propagandist and Novelist," *Studies in Philology,* XXIX (1932), 176-199.
3. Cf. Lewis Hanke, *Bartolomé de Las Casas: Bookman, Scholar, & Propagandist* (Philadelphia, 1952), pp. 37-81.
4. V. T. Harlow (ed.), *The Discoverie of the Large and bewtiful Empire of Guiana.,* By Walter Raleigh. (London, 1928), p. 21.
5. *Ibid.,* p. 66.
6. Wright, *Religion and Empire,* pp. 113-114.

CHAPTER II

1. Thomas Hariot, *A briefe and true report of the new found land of Virginia* (1588), Sigs. A4 verso—B1.
2. *Ibid.,* Sig. B1 verso.
3. William Strachey, *The Historie of Travaile Into Virginia Britannia.* Ed. R. H. Major, The Hakluyt Society (London, 1849), p. 120.
4. Louis B. Wright, *The First Gentlemen of Virginia* (San Marino, California, 1940), p. 301.
5. John Smith, *The Generall Historie of Virginia, New England, & The Summer Isles* (Glasgow, 1907), I, 61.
6. Quoted in Wright, *Religion and Empire,* p. 95.
7. Philip Alexander Bruce, *Economic History of Virginia in the Seventeenth Century* (New York, 1907), I, 240-241.
8. *Ibid.,* I, 211.
9. Sig. a3 verso.
10. Wright, *First Gentlemen of Virginia,* p. 106.
11. James E. Gillespie, *The Influence of Oversea Expansion on England to 1700* (New York, 1920), p. 48.
12. *Ibid.,* p. 48.
13. *Ibid.,* p. 109.

CHAPTER III

1. A part of this first appeared in Louis B. Wright, "The Westward Advance of the Atlantic Frontier," *The Huntington Library Quarterly*, XI (1948), 261-275.

2. *The First Explorations of the Trans-Allegheny Region by the Virginians, 1650-1674*, ed. Clarence W. Alvord and Lee Bidgood (Cleveland, Ohio, 1912), pp. 112-113.

3. *Memoirs of a Huguenot Family*, ed. Ann Maury (New York, 1872), pp. 288-289.

4. Richmond C. Beatty and William J. Mulloy (eds.), *William Byrd's Natural History of Virginia or The Newly Discovered Eden* (Richmond, Va., 1940), pp. 11, 14.

5. *Ibid.*, pp. 2-3.

6. *Ibid.*, p. 33.

7. *Ibid.*, p. 35.

8. Alexander S. Salley, Jr. (ed.), *Narratives of Early Carolina, 1650-1708* (New York, 1911), p. 207.

9. *Ibid.*, p. 208.

10. Lewis C. Gray and Esther K. Thompson, *History of Agriculture in the Southern United States* (Washington, D. C., 1933), I, 278; quoted from the *Calendar of State Papers, America and West Indies, 1677-1680*, p. 59.

11. *Ibid.*, I, 278-279.

12. *Ibid.*, I, 290.

13. *Ibid.*, I, 292.

14. James A. Williamson, *The Ocean in English History* (Oxford, 1941), p. 107.

15. Gray & Thompson, *History of Agriculture*, I, 184. See also *Ibid.*, II, 680 ff.

16. J. Max Patrick (ed.), *Azilia: A Discourse by Sir Robert Montgomery, 1717, Projecting a Settlement in the Colony Later Known as Georgia*, Emory University Publications: Sources and Reprints, Series IV (Atlanta, 1948), p. 18.

17. *Ibid.*, p. 18.

18. *Ibid.*, p. 23.

19. *Ibid.*, p. 12.

20. Verner W. Crane, *The Southern Frontier, 1670-1732* (Durham, N. C., 1928), p. 280.

21. E. Merton Coulter, *Georgia; A Short History* (Chapel Hill, N. C., 1947), pp. 17-18.

22. Verner W. Crane, "A Lost Utopia of the First American Frontier," *Sewanee Review*, XXVII (1919), pp. 48-61.

Index